FIRST ROUNDUP
WESTERN BALLADS

Written and Illustrated
By
Dee Strickland Johnson

ACKNOWLEDGMENTS:

My appreciation to my husband John (without whose encouragement the poems herein would still be residing in a notebook) and my daughter Becky, proof reader extraordinary. Thanks also to Elaine Filion for allowing me to use the drawing "Bill's Boots," the original of which she is the owner. (Portrait acknowledgments appear in the Index on page 55).

A MATTER OF ETHICS:

When I first began to recite poetry at cowboy gatherings, I was surprised when someone would occasionally ask, "Who wrote that poem?" To me it seemed perfectly obvious that if a person had recited a poem without acknowledgment, the poem was original. I was later to learn, however, that this is not necessarily true. It should be. By neglecting acknowledgment, a presenter leaves the impression that a piece is his/her own. This is, to me, right up there with cattle rustlin' -- maybe even with horse theft, fer cryin' out loud! I have always believed cowboys to be among the finest of gentlemen, and to those who recite poems I say:
1) Secure permission from the author before reciting a poem.
2) <u>Always</u> give the author's name immediately before presenting the piece. 3) When an artist is engaged for pay, doing another poet's copyrighted work without permission is clearly illegal. But legality is not the question. It's a matter of ethics.

Printed by Bierl Printing, Inc.
First Printing

Copyright © 1997 by Dee Strickland Johnson
HC 3, Box 593F, Payson, AZ 85541
Library of Congress Catalog Card Number: 97-92593
All rights reserved.

ISBN# 0-929526-79-1

Published by Double B Publications
4123 N. Longview Ave.
Phoenix, Arizona 85014
602-274-7236

DEDICATED TO

my father Troy Strickland, from whom I learned my first cowboy songs and whose gifts of joy and singing were a blessing to all who knew him.

"He was the mountain of my life;
 he was my dad."

. . . Chester James

Table of Contents

I. **Barroom Ballads** (7)
   The Dark Eyed Stranger 8
   Not Quite Lost Weekend............... 10
   Rawhide Annie 11
   Deja Vu 12
   Queen of Spades 14
   The Quiet Man 17

II. **"Literarier" (?) Stuff** (19)
   Morning in the High Hills 20
   Winds of the West 21
   My Blue Eyed Anna Beth 22
   Fredonia 24
   Cowboy Poetry: Out of Style 26

III. **Dang Fool Nonsense** (29)
   First Roundup 30
   The Boston Horse Trader 32
   The Taming of Wild Cat Willie 34
   At the Dance 36
   The Really Rich Rancher 38
   Tom's Truck 40
   My Buddy 44
   These Boots *Ain't* Made for Walkin' 47

IV. **Long Trail Winding** (49)
   My Vanishing Boots and Hats 50
   Cowboy Goes A-Courtin' 51
   Passing of a Cowboy 54
   The Secret 56
   The Blind Cowboy 59
   End of the Day 62

V. **Index** 63

"The Dark-Eyed Stranger"

Barroom Ballads

". . . a goodly crowd was there which well nigh filled Joe's barroom at the corner of the square."

. . . H. Antoine D'Arcy, <u>The Face Upon the Floor</u>

THE DARK-EYED STRANGER

He came to Globe one Friday night,
    the town was open wide.
He rode up to the *Bucket of Blood*
    and tied his horse outside.
A woman's voice rang clear and sweet
    above the reckless din;
The stranger leaned against the bar
    and told the keeper, "Gin!"

He turned his eyes toward the girl
    all painted shamelessly;
In dress of red, she tossed her head
    the singing lady Lee.
As cold and hard his dark-eyed glance
    and stern unsmiling lips
As the silver-handled six-gun
    hanging low upon his hip.

Now Lee could smile with crimson lips
    that meant a great deal more.
She touched his arm, he turned away
    and started for the door.
A man called Gus reached for the girl;
    she cried out, twisting free.
He lunged and leered and laughing loud,
    he pulled her to his knee.

He joked and jeered and gestured
    toward the stranger at the door.
A bullet flashed, a bottle crashed,
    and Gus lay on the floor.
The girl stood still, afraid to move,
    and no one made a sound.
The stranger turned his back to go,
    then slowly looked around.

The silver-handled gun he slid
    along the bar to Lee,
At last he spoke, the silence broke,
    said, "Sing your songs for me!"

Though many years have passed
    since then,
Still out on Murphy's Mound,
There lives a lonely lady
    who seldom comes to town.

She's proud, and prim and proper,
    she's a pious thing of grace,
But no man's ever dared to set
    his foot upon her place.

They say she speaks to not a man;
    she's waiting for someone.
She wears a pink sunbonnet
    and a silver-handled gun.

He took her heart
    did the dark eyed stranger,
Took it from its sordid path of sin.
He still has her heart,
    has the dark-eyed stranger,
Though he never passed that way again.

ΩΩΩΩΩ

... Dee Strickland, © 1959, 1997

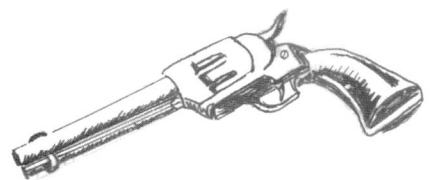

(The next two poems are based on favorite jokes that I've known for years. The first one is an old Scottish tale).

NOT QUITE LOST WEEKEND

J. D. Maxwell worked near Keams Canyon
   on a ranch called the *Rockin' XA.*
With his horse as his only companion,
   he started for Flagstaff one day.

He spent the whole weekend cavortin'
   where most of the young cowboys go --
The bars 'round that spit and cuss corner
   across from the railroad depot.

He started home Monday, past midnight;
   kept tiltin' his weavin' head back,
A bottle tipped up, still a-drinkin',
   Though the night was plumb starless
      and black.

He'd progressed well nigh into a gallop,
   though he thought he was still at a walk,
When a prairie dog hole tripped his horse up,
   and J.D. was throwed on a rock.

When he come to, he'd sobered up slightly;
   and feelin' his thunderin' head,
Said that reckless young
   hard drinkin' cowboy,
"With a headache like this, I ain't dead!"

But his hand had been dampened
   by somethin'.
Had he heard that bottle go *"thud?"*
   And, anxious, he tasted his fingers;
"Hot dang!" he yelled, *"It's only blood!"*

ΩΩΩΩΩ

. . . *Dee Strickland Johnson,* © *July, 1995*

RAWHIDE ANNIE

We called her Rawhide Annie;
She was big and bad and tough --
Except when she was drinkin' --
Then she didn't seem so rough.

She owned a ranch out west of town;
Ran a hundred head or more;
And no one crossed old Annie,
For she packed a forty-four!

She could rope and ride and lie and cuss
The way all cowhands can.
In her Levi's, boots, and grubby hat,
She looked just like a man.

One Friday night she came to town
And stopped for a few stiff shots,
Till the barkeep called, "Five minutes, Gents,
Five more is all you've got!"

We hangers-on all tossed 'em down
And were puttin' on our coats
When, from the far end of the bar,
Annie loudly cleared her throat.

She announced while peeping
    in her hands
That she'd cupped in a kind of dome,
"The guy who names what's in my hands,
Will get to take me home!"

A loud guffaw and a wry voice called,
"A big bad long horn steer!"
"Whoa!" cried Ann, peeking in her hands,
 "We got a winner here!"
      ΩΩΩΩΩ

   . . . *Dee Strickland Johnson,* © *May, 1995*

DÉJÀ VU

The lady hesitated with her hand
    on the barroom door.
'Twas thirty years since that awful night
    when she'd been inside before;
But 'twas over ten days
    since she'd seen her man,
Who'd been out on a rambling roam;
So she swallowed her pride and stepped inside --
    she had come to bring him home.

The kid at the tinkly piano,
    his sleeves gartered up with red bands,
Was tickling the keys in a fashion so free
That the liquid notes leapt from his hands.
The room was a riot of ruckus,
    and great clouds of blue smoke rolled.
The place was a din, and someone within
Yelled, "Hey, Eddie! Play somethin' old!"

The lady looked toward the piano,
    and she took it all in at a glance.
She seemed slightly to sway,
    as she started that way;
And she moved in a sort of a trance.
She observed the youth's fingers dancing
    on the black and ivory keys,
 His quick easy grace, and the lines of her face
    seemed to soften, her tension to ease.

⟶

Now Eddie, seeing the lady,
    and aware of her silent esteem,
Sent a shower of sound
    cascading around
    like a fountain of shimmering dreams.
He was certain she didn't frequent
    this god-forsaken place.
In his two years or more,
    he'd not seen before
        this gentle and lady-like face.

She might have been his mother,
    or his father's sister Bess,
Who had kindly loaned him money,
    when he'd planned to come out West.
So he smiled and played with flourish
    yet another old time tune,
        and he knew she recognized it --
        Roll along, Kentucky Moon.

The tune seemed to sober her husband,
    and it seemed to rub him wrong,
For he said with a grin,
    "They're flirtin' again,.
    And he's playin' that same damn song!"
This bleary eyed man, a wavering hand
    Unsteadily started to lower.
A roar and a flash! A discordant crash!
    and the kid slowly slumped to the floor;

His blood trickled over the ivories
    and silenced the bottles and dice,
"Damn, you, Joe!" screamed the one
    with the still smoking gun,
"Now you've made me kill you twice!"

ΩΩΩΩΩ

. . . Dee Strickland Johnson, © June, 1995

THE QUEEN OF SPADES

You've heard lots of songs
   'bout the queen of hearts
And the queen of diamonds too,
   But this one here's 'bout the
   Queen of Spades
I'm about to sing to you.

The territory's most beautiful face
   Drove men to wild charades,
And account of the graves
   that were dug 'cause of her,
We called her the *Queen of Spades.*

Yes, she was the reason for many a corpse
   That lay mouldering out on Boot Hill,
For many men fought, and many men died;
   Each time we said, "More prob'ly will!"

The kind of woman makes men go mad
   Where women are pretty damn scarce;

⎯⎯⎯→

And it don't really matter if good or bad,
    A man will go back if he dares.

Her hair was black, and her eyes were green,
    And her heart was as gray as lead;
She looked every bit the role of a queen
    For which many a man lay dead.

She had emeralds, diamonds, sapphires, and pearls,
She had clothes that you wouldn't believe,
So she could outshine us few prairie grass girls.
    She had suitors from lawyers to thieves.

They said she had a collection she prized --
    Like a cowboy will treasure his horse --
"A gallery of dead men's pictures!" they said,
    But I wouldn't know, of course.

"And in the corner of every last frame
    An old poker card parades - -
And the strangest thing is that every last one
    Is the same, -- it's the Queen of Spades!"

That short hitching rail come up missing one day
    -- Used to stand by her house in the shade,
Where the men would leave their horses tied
    While they called on the Queen of Spades.

They found her the very next Saturday,
    She lay sprawled upon her bed;
And nobody knew what had transpired,
    But the Queen of Spades was dead!

One of the pictures lay broken;
    Both the face and the card torn to shreds.
And the coroner called the cause of death
    "Blunt object to the head."

And that was confirmed by the bloody rail
    That was found amongst the shrubs;
But what told it best had been left on her breast --
    One card -- the Queen of Clubs!

ΩΩΩΩΩ

. . . *Dee Strickland Johnson,* © March 1995

"*He drank and the place was silent . . .*"

. . . The Quiet Man

(This is an old yarn which I told with pleasure for many years before writing it as a poem).

THE QUIET MAN

The stranger entered the tavern
   and ordered a shot of Red Eye.
"You're new around here, ain't you?"
   "Yep," was the stranger's reply.

He drank, and the place was silent,
   so the barkeep tried again;
"Well, what might your name be,
   Stranger?"
"Tex."
   Stillness.
      Then one word, "Gin."

"So you're from Texas, are you?"
   The stranger answered, "No."
"Not from Texas?"
"Nope."
   More silence.
      Stranger made as if to go.

"Then where, pray tell, do you hail from?"
   asked the barkeep, clearing his throat.
The stranger said, "Lou'siana,"
   stood up and put on his coat.

"Well, if you're from Louisiana,
   why're you called Tex, if you please?"
The reply was most emphatic,
   "Don't aim to be called *Louise*!"

ΩΩΩΩΩ

. . . Dee Strickland Johnson © November, 1996

" . . . rhythm and rhyme are 'passe' --
just 'poor Hudebrastic style.'"

. . . <u>Cowboy Poetry: Out of Style</u>

"Literarier"(?)Stuff

"O bards of rhymeless meter free,
My gratitude goes out to ye
For all your deathless lines -- ahem!
Let's see now. . . . what is one of them?"

... Franklin Pierce Adams,
<u>To a Vers Librist</u>

MORNING IN THE HIGH HILLS

In the quietness of morning
    when the sky is clear and white
        and dawn's soft hush has slipped
            across the solitude of night,
When the last pale star has fallen
    and a gentle, warming sun
        heralds yesterday's tomorrow,
            I know today has newly come.

There is nothing quite so moving,
    quite so silent, quite so strange
        as the Lord's most recent wonder --
            birth of morning on the range.
Then I nearly burst with gladness,
    fill with ecstasy and pride
        at the vast wide open spaces
            from the faithful horse I ride.

I just can't quite seem to fathom --
    I just can't help wondering why
        I was placed amongst such beauty --
            all this solitude and sky.
Then I watch the God of sunrise
    spread the day across the earth
        with a quiet breath of blessing
            and a whisper of His mirth.

$$\Omega\Omega\Omega\Omega\Omega$$

. . . Dee Strickland Johnson, © *August, 1993*

(Words are wonderful. This is a poetic lark with language).

WINDS OF THE WEST

Wind, wind, winds of the west,
Vague voices call from the land I love best.
Sighing and crying and hauntingly free,
Incessantly whistling and whisp'ring to me.

No matter how far or how often I roam
O'er vast verdant fields or the dark ocean's foam,
I'll never find freedom; I'll never find rest,
While the wild wind is wantonly willing me west.

The warm winds of summer are singing to me.
The breezes blow fresh'ning and fragrant
   and free;
And no matter where or how far I may be,
The winds of the west will keep calling to me.

Wind, wind, wild western wind,
Haunting me, wanting me westward again.
Taunting, undaunting, wherever I roam --
Exciting, delighting, inviting me home.

Echoes of voices that sang long ago
Still willing me westward, calling me home.
Sun, sand, and sagebrush, saguaro and pine,
Cottonwood, piñon; the west is all mine.

The wild winds of winter wail warning to me:
I must come back home. Its a great mystery
From where canyons cut deep
   and the wastelands are wide,
The winds of the west never seem to subside.

Wind, wind, wild western winds
Summon me back to the saddle again.
No matter where or how far I may be,
The winds of the west will keep calling to me.
    The winds of the west wail,
      "Come home! Home to me!"
       ΩΩΩΩΩ

... Dee Strickland Johnson © April, 1997

(This poem is dedicated to my parents, Anna and Troy Strickland, on whose lives it is based. It begins with a quotation from Poe's Annabel Lee, my mother's favorite poem).

MY BLUE EYED ANNA BETH

*"It was many and many a year ago
In a kingdom by the sea,
That a maiden there lived whom you may know
By the name of Annabel Lee;
And this maiden she lived with no other thought
Than to love and be loved by me."*

It was many and many a summer day
'Neath a greenlit aspen tree,
That my sweetheart, my blue-eyed Anna Beth,
First read that sweet poem to me;
And it was the first of many a verse;
Still, none was so sweet as she.

She called me her *"handsome young cowboy lad"*
As she rode close by my side,
Her *"rollicking, frolicking cowboy lad,"*
Her *"darling,"* her *"pleasure,"* her *"pride."*
And together we rode the familiar trails,
And I asked her to be my bride.

It was many and many an autumn night
That we sat by the fireside's glow,
While flickering lights in her blue eyes bright
From the flames glanced to and fro.
There she read, and she sang to my old guitar
And our love continued to grow.

⟶

It was many and many a winter eve,
When the winds cut like a knife,
That we wandered a forest of snow-clad pine,
I and my fair young wife;
And we talked of the child that was to be,
Of the beat of a new heart's life.

It was many a Spring that the fair sweet child,
With her eyes of piñon brown
And her golden curls falling free and wild,
Caught the blossoms that drifted down.
And Anna Beth wove them into a wreath;
And the child wore a wood sprite's crown.

Something silent and strange
    then crept over the range,
And a blight soon fell over the rose,
And the child's precious face
    it quite soon did erase,
And I watched as her eyelids closed.
Then on the sweet breath
    of my dear Anna Beth
Were no songs and no verses
    but hinted of death.
Now I ride, all alone, the long trail.
    Two graves by the long lonely trail.

ΩΩΩΩΩ

. . . Dee Strickland Johnson, © May, 1995

(Note: The sister I never knew died at the age of three. Some people said that my mother, who passed away a few years later, died of a broken heart).

FREDONIA

(Quite unintentionally after Robert Frost)

I saddle up one afternoon,
    and happily I hum the tune
        of some old plaintive cowboy song.
As if to say I'd got it wrong,
    Fredonia shakes her mane and head,
        and I believe she's firmly said,
            "Cut the horseplay! Let's get on
                the timber trail. Forget the song."

The trail winds upward, twisting, rising
    toward the west where, with surprising
        artistry, the sun, in leaving,
    shafts of light and shade is weaving --
        purple, gold and crimson bright --
            with harmonizing
                shades of night.

Among the white-barked aspen trees,
    I touch the reins and press my knees
        against her sides. Fredonia halts
            and turns to know if she's at fault.
I dismount to lie among
    the fallen leaves -- once green and young,
        now old and brown.
            They cushion me as I lie down.

Fredonia flicks her tail to say,
    "Get up! We must be on our way!"
The cooling dampness holds me still.
    Fredonia's eyes are on the hill.
        I rise, reluctantly, and mount
            the little mare
                who really thinks
                      we're bound somewhere.

ΩΩΩΩΩ

. . . Dee Strickland Johnson, © *July, 1995*

"Fredonia"

(Cowboy poetry has been criticized as "doggerel." Here a cowboy quotes 18th century poet Alexander Pope's criticism of "modern" unrhymed and unmetered verse).

COWBOY POETRY: OUT OF STYLE

They say rhythm and rhyme are *"passe"* --
    they're just *"poor Hudebrastic style."*
Despite the fact that it's <u>tough</u> to rhyme,
    they say, *"macaronics -- quite juvenile!"*
I propose to compose here a lyric
    in free or blankety-blank verse;
And you, when the effort is over,
Tell me which of my wordings is w . . . .
    inferior to the other.

(Here goes!):
    Ol' Cookie gets up before daylight,
        despite his long hours of toiling;
    He kicks at the various bedrolls
        as soon as the coffee is b . . .
        beginning to brew in the spacious
        blackened receptacle.

Next up is the faithful ol' wrangler;
    he's out there a-checkin' each horse.
Then the cowboys roll out from their
    soogans;
They're right anxious for breakfast, of c...
    bacon and sour dough biscuits and
        jerky gravy and numerous particles
        of Arizona sand.

A cowboy's mind gets to wanderin'
    as his horse calmly grazes the grass;
A rabbit jumps up, his pony bucks,
    and throws the poor sap on his a . . .
    derriere -- to whence he has been
        propelled by the violent upheaval
        of the ejection.

They ride and they cuss and they circle;
    as the heat waves increase, they sag.
A hot wind blows; the dust clouds roll --
    its just awful if you're ridin' dr . . .
    in back of the cattle, sort of
        "bringing up the rear" as it were.

The minutes crawl by
   and the hours and days,
      and you haven't shaved in a week,
And when you eventually get into town,
   people stare -- as if you was some fr . . .
      extremely unusual being,
      perhaps from outer space.

You get a bath, a shave, and a haircut;
   and you feel like you're in a trance:
New shirt, clean Levi's, a boot shine,
   and you head for some good cowboy d . . .
      frolic -- at which the gentlemen
      rhythmically spin their partners
      in time to melodic harmonies
      produced by a variety
      of musical instruments.

You dance as close as you can to the band;
   get a thrill right there in your middle,
A-holdin' that red-headed gal real tight,
   as you sway to the git-tar and fi . . .
      violin.

Ah, come on! I've had enough of this;
   and so have you, I hope!
This ain't "poetry but prose run mad."
   (I quote the late Alexander P . . .
   what's his name --
You know, that great English poet
   of the Augustin age who
   "polished the heroic couplet until
      it sparkled with brilliance").

Take me back to my boots and *doggerel,*
My scribbles, and saddles, and rope!
   I'll write of a *frogerrel*
   who sat on his *loggerel.*
   Give us *rhyme* anytime,
        Eh, Mr....(uh) *Pope!*?

ΩΩΩΩΩ

. . . Dee Strickland Johnson, © *October, 1996*

'We poets are (upon a poet's word)
Of all mankind the creatures most absurd."

. . . Alexander Pope

Dang Fool Nonsense

"There is a foolish corner in the brain
of the wisest man."

. . . Aristotle

This poem is dedicated to Bob Koch who suggested it one chilly night after observing the author with booted feet "might nigh in the campfire."

FIRST ROUNDUP

Come gather around, all you cowhands;
    I'll tell you the tale of a squall,
All about the very first roundup
    By the very first cowboy of all.
They called this here ol' waddie *Shorty*,
    Though his real name was *Noah* or *Pop*;
This honest old pard found times were hard,
    Though he'd dealt all *his* cards from the top.

Boss said, *"You're a good puncher, Shorty;*
    And seein's how you've stood the big test,
I'm securin' you and your fam'ly;
    And I'm cuttin' out all the rest.
Go build a gargantuan stable,
    Gather critters from both land and sky. . . ."
So Shorty completed that roundup --
    As per them commands from on high,

The rains came and flooded the country;
    No range land -- just H2 and O.
A couple of days and his daughter
    Called, *"Quick, Pop! There's a leak in the hold!"*
He hurried down, investigatin';
    "Woe is me! I fear this is the end!"
And that's when the very first cowboy
    Learned which beast was to be his best friend!

For the dog stuck his snout in the puncture;
    And his mate took her turn at the hole.
And together they staved off destruction,
    And saved every body and soul;

⟶

But the gap grew too large for their noses!
    Shorty came to his pals' frantic bark;
"Oh how," he cried out in anguish,
    "Can we, dearest wife, save the ark?"

His sweet little spouse to the rescue!
    To forestall any great avalanche,
She stuck her left heel in the puncture
    And saved their amphibious ranch.

The animals wailed in misgiving;
    With grunt, and with snort, and with bleat,
For the hole only kept getting bigger,
    Though she plugged it with both of her feet!

A fortnight had passed when his helpmate
    Cried, *"We've simply got to acquire*
Some sort of stopper or stuffing,
    Or we're all of us bound to expire!"

Well, Shorty just did what he had to --
    He hurried back down in the hold;
He slogged through the chill rising water
    And sat himself down on the hole.

Nearly three weeks he sat with his backside
    Exposed to the sea -- unrefined!
While minnows and oysters and lobsters
    Took a swipe at ol' Shorty's behind.

Then the white dove flew out and returned with
    The leaf of an olive tree rare.
The sun shone, a rainbow glowed glorious,
    And Shorty withdrew his damp derriere.

Now that is the true explanation
    How the dog his cold nose did acquire;
Why ladies complain of cold tootsies,
    And cowboys back up to the fire!

ΩΩΩΩΩ

    . . . . *Dee Strickland Johnson,* © *October, 1996*

THE BOSTON HORSE TRADER

Harry's a horseman who comes from back east;
There's nothing that he doesn't know
    'bout the beast --
Or that's what he's certain to tell you, at least,
That mighty horse trader from Boston.

Can't tell a cow's head from a horses' rear end;
He thinks *palomino's* his Mexican friend;
A *stud* is a tie tack that's up with the trend;
A good hat's by old J.B. ***stallion.***

Now a ***quarter horse*** is his joy and his pride --
(He drops in two bits for a hell of a ride!)
A ***buckskin's*** a masculine deer's outside,
And ***broncos*** and ***mustangs*** drink Chevron.

A ***sorrel's*** a grief, and a ***pinto's*** a bean,
A ***paint*** is for changin' the red barn to green,
A ***chestnut's*** a sucker for knights, rooks,
    and queen --
Thinks the mighty horse trader from Boston.

Dun means *all finished*; the sky is a ***blue;***
A ***bay*** is an inlet the sea runs into.
Filly's a dress with a ruffle or two;
A ***gray's*** a confederate soldier.

He thinks that ***mare*** means *in addition to*;
A ***gelding*** is something of rich golden hue;
A ***colt*** is a gun that the movie stars use
In old *shoot 'em up* B-grade westerns.

A ***strawberry roan*** is something you eat;
A good ***appaloosa's*** another big treat;
A ***black's*** from New Orleans --
    hot spicy burnt meat;
Thoroughbred is whole wheat --
    made by *Holsom.*

⎯⎯➤

A *donkey's* an engine; a *jack* is a fish.
Burro: frijole-filled Mexican dish.
A *mule* is a slipper that goes "slide" and "slish"
A *jenny* is kind of a spinster.

So if you're a-wantin' to buy a good steed,
Don't reckon this trader's
　　the merchant you need.
Don't believe what you hear!
　　Get a warrantee deed
From that mighty horse trader from Boston!

ΩΩΩΩΩ

. . . *Dee Strickland Johnson,* © *May, 1997*

THE TAMING OF WILD CAT WILLIE

Sure you've heard of Wild Cat Willie,
    The worst, meanest hombre of all!
That notorious gun-slinging outlaw
    Who carried a whole arsenal!

I was drinkin' a sars'parilly
    At a place called *Hortensia's Bar.*
When the door come a-bustin' wide open
    And ol' Wild Cat was planted right thar!

Now he was a man of a mountain!
    Ur . . . a monument of a mig mup. . .
It theems that sust-binkin'-athout it,
    My tort-songue-of-tits-gwetsed up!

He was BIG! And this light was a-burnin'
    Like fire in his eyes! I could see
Them fuses was short, and him glarin'
    And starin' them right straight at me!

He hollered, "Dude, what *are* you a-drinkin'?"
    "Ulp!" (My knees felt like papery pulp).
"Pour this durn fool some Red Eye!" He bellowed.
    "Now *you* drink that down in one gulp!"

He was encouragin' me with them wild eyes
    And the barrel of his forty-four Colt.
I tossed her right down and got blowed up
    By a jolt like this huge thunderbolt!

I just laid there -- till I heard quite clearly,
    Someone sayin', "We thought you was dead!"
(I'd just slipped in my sars'parilly;
    Hell, that whiskey went straight to my head!)

——▶

But where was that mean Wild Cat Willie?
He had been there just seconds before!
When I slipped in my sars'parilly --
Wild Cat Willie'd got smashed by the door!

My spurred boot had slammed
    that big door shut,
Though *I* wasn't much hurt by the fall.
I helped them unplaster old Willie.
We just peeled him right off of the wall!

He was flattened and long -- like a noodle!
He stood well above seven feet high!
That is, he would've if'n he could've --
But his wild rag was caught in his fly!

His nose was squnched up like a porker,
While his voice, quite ferocious before,
When he started to speak,
    sounded like a high squeak,
Where before, it was more like a roar.

Now, he didn't look quite so fright'nin';
I decided right then and there that
I'd send him back home to my mama
'Cause I promised I'd get her a *flat*!

That's the tale of old Wild Cat Willie,
How I knocked the wind out of his sails.
I caught that tough
    by the scruff of the ruff,
And that's how I end this cat's tail!

ΩΩΩΩΩ

. . . Dee Strickland Johnson © September, 1995

(This is another example of the fun a poet can have just playing with words).

AT THE DANCE

I's feelin' right lonesome, so I rode into town,
Just like some dang stranger a-lookin' around.
I heard music playin'; it looked like a dance,
So I tethered ol' Lightnin';
    sez, "I'll take a chance."
Then I was right happy I hadn't no pals,
For the place was plumb filled up
       with good lookin' gals!

There was Callie and Hallie and Sally and Sue,
Molly and Dolly and Polly and Lou.
There was Carrie and Mary
    and Sherry and Bea,
And Lilly and Millie and Tilly and Dee.
In come Mandy and Candy
    and Tandy and Jan,
Marilyn, Carolyn, Carol and Ann.

This cow puncher figured
    he'd sure won the prize!
There was tall ones and small ones --
      most every last size!
I was sure in a quandary, just wonderin' which
To ask first to dance with,
    and when I should switch,

When I heard a commotion
    just outside the door;
Such a passel of cowboys, I'd not seen before!
Then Randy snatched Candy,
    and Andy took Sue.
Danny and Manny and Stanley and Stu
Snagged Callie and Carol and Lilly and Lou.

                                  →

Mary and Carrie with Barry and Hal
Were trippin' fantastic like Larry and Sal.
Dan danced with Carolyn, Jerry took Ann,
Gary with Marilyn, Dolly with Van.
Tandy and Mandy swung onto the floor
With Johnny and Ronnie;
    then in come some more.

Millie copped Micky,
    but she danced with Nick
Who was cut in by Ricky,
    and I's feelin' sick;
For Harry whirled Hallie
    and Perry twirled Bea.
I's eyein' Molly, while Polly eyed me.
Then Billy tagged Tilly,
    and Willie grabbed Dee,
And silly old Sammy
    snitched Molly from me.

Barry nabbed Sherry,
    and Jay winked at Jan.
But one woman left --
    and me the last man.
Them durn frisky punchers
    had took all the rest,
But dang, if they hadn't gone
    left me the best --
That perky pink Polly --
    she's pretty and plump.
She's my kind of woman --
    so I held the trump!

ΩΩΩΩΩ

. . . *Dee Strickland Johnson,* © *June, 1995*

THE REALLY RICH RANCHER AND ME

Last weekend I met a rich man --
   owns a million head or more:
Angus and Brangus -- and *horses*:
   Arabians by the score.
An O-lympic pool and six bathrooms,
   ten thousand square feet of space --
And that is for only him and his wife
   and the maid that helps
      keep up the place.

And all of that really ain't nothin'!
Why, I thought I'd seen a mirage
    when I got a peek at his "carriage house"
      as well as his three car garage.
A new Bronco in the latter
   (for slummin' and mendin' fence),
A Rolls -- sorta misty metallic gray,
    and a shiny green Mercedes Benz.

There's a tan '31 Plymouth Roadster
   and a powder blue '38 Cord,
An El Dorado-Cadillac-hardtop,
    and most of the rest was Fords:
Like that '64-and-a-half yellow Mustang
   with four-on-the-floor-syncro-gears,
And three 1950's red T-Birds --
   one each of the three classic years.

I got in my rattle trap pickup,
   half Chevy, half Toy-ota yet!
(I call the durn thing a *Chevrota*,
   'Cause I don't like to say *Toy-o-let*).
Well, I drove that wreck back out to my place --
   Less'an seventeen acres dry ground,
With the outhouse out back of the woodshed;
   six or eight of the kids runnin' 'round.

I was ponderin' that rich feller's holdin's,
    and I told my sweet little wife;
She just hugged me and whispered,
    "Now Honey,
        what's *really important* in life?
"*Its happiness* really matters.
    Do you think all his money
        could buy it?"
Well, I don't really know
    if it can or it can't --
But I'd sure as hell like to try it!

ΩΩΩΩΩ

... Dee Strickland Johnson, © *October, 1995*

TOM'S TRUCK

With my horse on the fritz, and me needin' a Schlitz,
    I borried my brother-'n-law's truck.
I went on a bender and dented a fender --
    now ain't that a cow puncher's luck?
My pal Dick and me, we just went on a spree
    which lasted til three in the mornin';
Don't know about Dick, but I's feelin' right sick,
    when up comes this tree without warnin'!

Well, I drove that ol' Dodge in that spavined garage
    out back of my brother-'n-law's diggin's.
I just borried his tools and started to fool
    with my own "cowboy's best" jerry-riggin's.
I was pushin' my luck, but since it was *his* truck,
    I didn't feel I was encroachin'.
I was hammerin' out dents with thoughts so intense,
    I didn't hear no one approachin'.

I was doin' right well; 'least I's workin' like hell --
    no one could say I wasn't tryin'!
When I heard this wild roar comin' in at the door
    like the scream of a mad mountain lion.
I tore out the back way; (it was just gettin' day,
    and I didn't have time for no gear);
I jumped on my horse -- which was ailin', of course,
    and I hollered, "Let's get out of here!

"You just better get well, or we're headed for hell,
    that ol' brother-'n-law sure ain't a-foolin'!"
I lit outta town, took the long way aroun'
    so Tom's temper'd have time to be coolin'.
My throat was plumb dry and no water was nigh
    (It was smack in the middle of summer),
Headin' back to the ranch when a low hangin' branch
    just landed me splat on my bummer!

Well, I bruised my back side (as well as my pride)
    but I scurried right up through the brambles;
My horse it was gone, but I hurried right on;
    through the mesquite and catclaw I scrambled.
I was covered with spines like a dang porcupine;
    I was cussin' and wishin' for water --
And that cayuse of mine; but minus my twine,
    I had no chance at all to have caught her!

Well, I didn't know why, but it seemed my right eye
    was a-achin', a swellin' was risin';
My Levi's was tore; an' my feet was right sore --
    (these boots ain't fer peedestri'izin'!)
I got down to my socks, creepin' over the rocks
    when I heard that ol' truck motor roarin'.
It was runnin' on wrath;
    'cause there warn't no cowpath --
Through the boondocks that ol' Dodge was soarin'!

I dived over a boulder and busted my shoulder,
    but leastwise, I'd got out of sight now,
As that pickup flew by, I fell in cow pie,
    which not greatly enhanc-ed my plight now!
That ol' pickup sailed past; it was goin' so fast,
    I could hear them ol' tires just a-screamin';
I just barely glimpsed him, but Tom's face
    looked so grim,
I knowed that his blood was a-steamin'!

I'd twisted my neck, but I watched that ol' wreck
    disappear from off the horizon;
It flew down a canyon, 'long with its companion.
    Ol' Tom, are we through fraternizin'?
From where I was lyin', I could see the tack flyin'
    from out of the bed of that truck,
There was bridles and reins
    scattered over the plains,
But not Tom, so I reckoned he's stuck.

Tom's Truck - 3 -

My thumb was a-dangle at some freakish angle,
    My Pendleton shirt was a shame now!
My hat was all smashed up;
    nose bleedin' and bashed up,
But I reckoned there's no one to blame now.
Then the ground, it turned blue, and when I come to,
    I looked like a tree with twelve branches.
The first one to call was that vet from Duvall
    who'd been makin' the rounds of the ranches.

He sez, "Your horse appears well, now how in the hell
    did *you* end up in the horsepital?"
I just laid there in bed and wished I was dead;
    I was achin' right more than a little.
He said, "That ol' waddie Stu from the ol' Flyin' U
    was the one that saved you from your doom.
He was mendin' a fence . . . . Oh, by coincidence,
    your brother-'n-law's in the next room!"

I sez,"You know a cowboy's right fond on his steed,
    but I think you might have some luck
Tryin' to borry his horse (ask politely, of course!) --
    just don't ask to borry his truck!"
The vet gave me a nip and at the first sip,
    my voice seemed to come from afar.
"When I get outta here, I'll be needin' a beer,
    So you and me'll go make the bars!

"I'll be well soon and we'll hit Jake's Saloon;
    then we'll move on to Black's and Lone Star.
Yeah, we'll pick ol' Dick up!
But Tom wrecked his ol' pickup,
    so we'll have to borry his car!"

ΩΩΩΩΩ

. . . Dee Strickland Johnson, © April, 1995

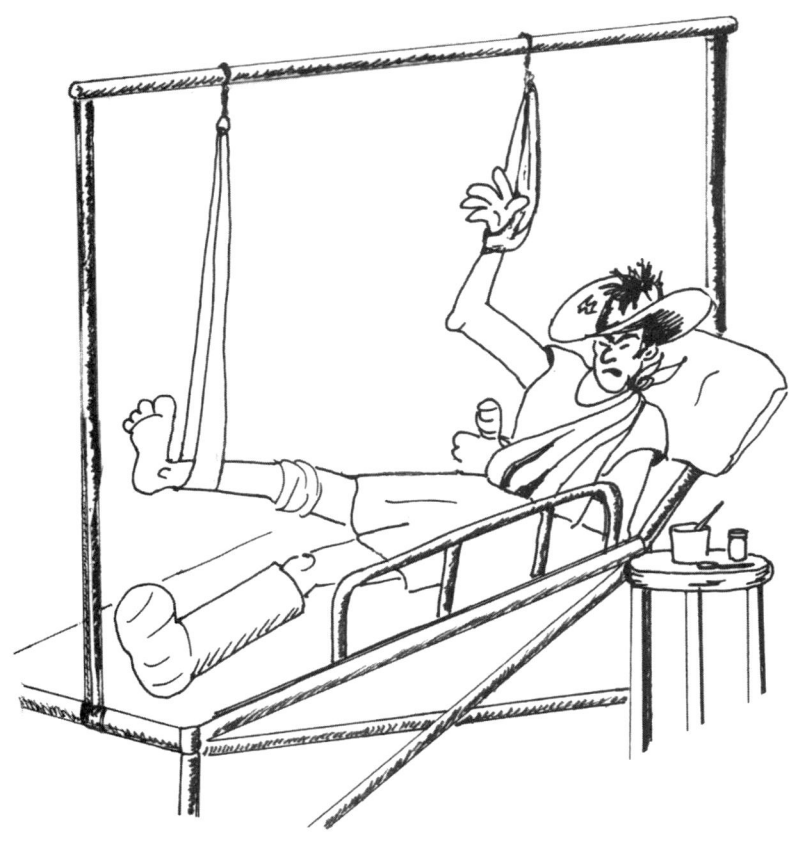

"Your horse appears well, now how in
the hell did <u>you</u> end up in the horsepital?"

. . . <u>Tom's Truck</u>

MY BUDDY

I've had a good buddy since high school,
We've pardnered through tough, thick, and thin;
And whenever I got into trouble,
    I knew that my buddy'd jump in.

He told me once he'd take care of the drinks,
    So he ordered two Coors and a cup;
Said I needed the beer to make gloom disappear
    And the coffee to sober me up.

When I came back inside from the boys' room,
    He just burped and then started to scold,
"I took care of your drinks,
    but your beer was quite warm,
        and your coffee was purt'n near cold!"

So I got stuck for the next round
    And the next and the next one or two,
By the time we decided to leave there,
    I reckon I'd had quite a few.

My buddy, he sure is a buddy!
    He lets me know where he stands,
Said, "A buddy don't let a buddy drive drunk!"
    And he took the keys out of my hand.

He helped me right into my pickup;
    Him and my girl got in the left side,
He said, "Yvonne will ride in the middle,
    You can handle the gates, and I'll drive!"

Well, we wound around out in the country;
    I got out to open a gate.
I just watched my old pickup pull through her.
    When I got her latched up, it'z too late!

⟶

My pickup was missin' a tail light;
    I just watched it recede out of sight.
"A long walk will sober you up, boy!"
    his voice floated back through the night.

I woke up 'round noon the next mornin',
    and thought maybe my missin' truck
Had landed right square of my Stetson;
    I felt like I'd been lightning struck!

I saddled ol' Blue and rode over
    to that ranch where my pal made his bunk.
I thanked him for savin' my pickup --
    maybe even my life -- 'cause I'uz drunk!

Why, he'd even took care of my girl friend,
    now that was especially kind!
He 'llowed's how it wasn't no trouble --
    he'd do it again any time!

Well, he didn't go back on that promise;
    every weekend he taken her home
When we all ended up there
    at *John's Place*
At the top of the street in Jerome.

One mornin' after a bender,
    I noticed he still had my keys,
My pickup was missin' a fender,
    and my Levi's had holes in the knees.

I decided I'd ought to take stock then
    just what had been goin' on;
It seemed like an awful long time since
    I'd been kissed good night by Yvonne.

So I saddled ol' Blue, and I lit out.
    I stood up to my buddy right well,
"Seems like you've been seein'
      a sight more of my girl
      than I've seen her myself for a spell!"

My buddy, he says, "May the best man win!"
    Well, I won that trick, I presume;
For by jokies, I turned out to be the best man!
    and my buddy -- well, he was the groom.

ΩΩΩΩΩ

. . . Dee Strickland Johnson
© June, 1996

(Note: At the time of the writing of this poem, a popular country western song was *These Boots are Made for Walkin'* -- a revival of the 1960's hit by Nancy Sinatra. Here an old cowboy begs to disagree with the singer).

THESE BOOTS *AIN'T* MADE FOR WALKIN'!

Say these boots are made for walkin'?
Now, that's plumb foolish talkin'!
Let's just trace that idle rumor to its source.
Any guy whose twelve or older,
With a saddle on his shoulder,
Will tell you straight, he's lookin' for a horse!

'Cause these boots ain't made for walkin'!
You just watch some cowboy rockin'
Like a sailor that's right newly come from sea.
Lest you want them tourists gawkin',
It's the *horse* should do the walkin'!
These boots are made for *ridin'*--'splain to see.

See, the toe here's kinda narrer,
That allows the footgear wearer
To slide easy in the stirrup when in haste;
And the heel's a little higher;
Now son, I ain't no liar,
That just locks your foot right down there
    into place!

They're made higher than your Reeboks--
Some comes might nigh to your knee box--
That protects your calves and shinbones
    from the brush.
Some dude says they're made for *walkin'*?
He's just ignorant or mockin',
You can set him straight or ask him please
    to hush.

When that sweet thing's up there singin'
While her voice is still a-ringin',
I could say, "Excuse me, honey,
    but you're wrong!
These boots are made for *ridin'*!" --
But there ain't no use collidin',
So, "Thank you, Ma'am, that's sure a nifty song!"
    ΩΩΩΩΩ

... Dee S. Johnson, © January 1996

"*The long trail's growing shorter,
 and the old trail's stretching back...*"

... Dee Strickland Johnson, <u>Trails</u>

Long Trail Winding

"... guide me on the long dim trail ahead
That stretches upward toward the Great Divide."

... Badger Clark, <u>A Cowboy's Prayer</u>

MY VANISHING BOOTS AND HATS
An Old Cowboy Contemplates

These boots are from Sears and Roebuck.
    This hat's from Montgomery Wards.
My beavers and leathers all vanished together --
    My stuff has just went by the boards!

These're made out of recycled cardboard --
    Or peach pits or kelp, I suspect,
Or yogurt or tofu; 'cause I certainly know who
    Don't find *me* environment'ly correct!

See, I'm livin' with my yuppie daughter;
    And it seems that in her quest for knowledge,
She's "lost" what I bought her,
    forgot all I taught her.
Lord, she's even goin' to *college*!

Now, regardin' my beat up *Resistol*,
    Justin boots, and old *Stetson* hat,
I ain't gettin' flurried; ain't too awful worried,
    'Cause, you see, I know right where they're at:

In the back of that upstairs closet,
    Where she thinks I won't ever look;
But I prowl around with my nose to the ground
    While she's got her nose in a book!

Yeah, and I've been observin' here lately,
    That "fake fur" she wears smells like mink!
And her *Birkenstocks* are
    might near on the rocks.
My stuff'll turn up soon here, I think!

ΩΩΩΩΩ

    . . . *Dee Strickland Johnson, © September, 1996*

COWBOY GOES A-COURTIN'

(This poem is based on the keen cowboy humor of Cephas Perkins of Perkins Valley, Holbrook, AZ. It is dedicated to Josie and Cephas, my "Mom and Pop").

My daddy died in '75.
Mom's been mighty lonesome since then;
But she's told me many and many a time,
"I'll never get married again!

"No one could take your daddy's place,
I'm not thinking of it at all!"
But then on the phone
   she casually mentioned --
That a cowboy had come to call.

It's that rancher Cephas Perkins --
Owns that big spread out west of town;
He'd taken her to dinner that week
And had sorta been hangin' around.

He's 80 years old and she's 82;
And both of 'em's spry as young foxes.
He don't hear too well,
   and she gets dizzy spells,
But they ain't hidin' out in no boxes!

Last Spring when I went to visit my mom,
I observed this progressing romance,
And to my way of observatin',
Old Cephas just might have a chance!

I said, "Cephas, why'd you
   leave your hat outside
On the bush by Mama's front door?"
(I'd noticed that every time he came,
He placed it right there as before).

⟶

"Well, if some other guy should come ridin' by,
   (I'm always suspectin' the worst),
When he's roundin' that curve,
   I want him to observe
That, by jingos, I got here first!"

"And how come it's always turned upside down?
   That protects the brim, I've no doubt."
"Well, I ain't concerned with the brim or the trim;
   I just don't want my luck to run out!"

"I hear you took Mom to the cattle auction
   Last week on the reservation."
"Yep! That's one hundred miles.
   Had to stop four times
     before we got back to the station."

"Four times! What's wrong with your pickup?"
   sez I.
Cephas laughs, "Tain't my truck!"
   Then he smiles,
"But a cowboy knows that when your gal goes,
   You get to kiss her each twenty miles!

"And to me it seems downright obvious
   that this match was made in heaven --
You know your Mama's four foot ten --
   Well, I'm four foot twenty-seven!"

Well, my Mom and Cephas
   got married last week,
And he told us with one of his grins,
"There's somethin' for shore
   to that old cowboy lore!
When a cowboy goes courtin', he wins!"

<u>ΩΩΩΩΩ</u>

. . . *Dee Strickland Johnson,* © *March, 1996*

"Sweethearts"

THE PASSING OF A COWBOY

(For my friend, Katie Burdette of Tennessee, who told me this tale)

Slim and Stumpy had been good partners
    since the days when names were shortened
'Cause questions weren't always healthy to ask,
    and it wasn't considered important.

They'd stuck together through thick and thin,
    just a couple of tough old sinners,
But these crusty old pards found times were hard,
    and both of them kept gettin' thinner.

Ol' Stumpy rode into town last week,
    just to see the "ediator"
Of the weekly Bumble Bee Tribune,
    'bout twelve o'clock or later.

"Now what can I do for you, Stumpy?"
    Stumpy lifted his eyes toward heaven,
And twisting that grubby old hat in his hands,
    said, "Cliff, Slim died this mornin' round seven."

Cliff pushed the green eye shade back on his brow;
    and he patted the bony old shoulder.
He recalled that he'd seen this old fellow last week,
    but today he looked twenty years older.
"You'll be wanting to put something in about Slim
    to let people know he's departed."
Cliff was taking the pencil from back of his ear,
    but Stumpy had already started:

"Sylvester Lassiter Isaac 'Slim' Moore --
    Put 'Slim' in them little do-hickies,
And use that darker sort of print --
    ol' Slim was always right picky.

⟶

"Sylvester Lassiter Isaac 'Slim' Moore --
   best pardner a man could draw,
Departed this vale . . . , No, make that 'trail'
. . . Oh, put 'He come from Arkansas.'"

Cliff cleared his throat, "It's five dollars a word,"
   Stumpy scratched his head, "That follers.
Then just write 'Slim's dead,'" the old man said,
   "I only got ten dollars."

"Look, I'll give you three words free, old Pal."
   Stumpy said, "Now, Cliff, you ortn't."
Cliff seeing his plight, said,"Stump, its all right;
   Now just write what's most important."

Stumpy was quiet, and his rheumy old eyes
   seemed gazing down some far off trail.
He pondered long; then in voice firm and strong,
   ol' Stumpy said, "Horse for sale!"

ΩΩΩΩΩ

. . . Dee Strickland Johnson © March, 1996

*(A Scottish lad comes to America and realizes
his dream of becoming a cowboy).*

THE SECRET

I headed out west at barely fifteen,
    and somehow I got hired on
To a cattle outfit;
    I's so proud I could spit
To be helpin' the cook before dawn.

I cut bacon from slabs,
    washed tin plates and pans,
And the gallons of water I'd tote!
I pulled brush and chopped limbs,
    filled cups to the brim
With java where horseshoes could float!

I thought I was macho
    as we camped by Picacho,
But *one thing* I could scarcely abide;
Yet it came with the work,
    which I sure didn't shirk --
Like learnin' to rope and to ride.

I took Cook's commands,
    and I made a good hand,
So the boss changed my job to
    horse wranglin'.
The work it was rough,
    and I sure acted tough;
Loved hearin' my own spurs a-janglin'!

They bit me, they kicked me,
    they stomped on my toes;
There's a scar from my cheek to my chin;

⟶

Got a twice-busted nose;
    but the hard way, I suppose,
Is the very best way to begin;
But there was *that one thing*
    that just stuck in my craw.
No one knew how hard it was for me!
'Cause I gritted and frowned,
    and I swallered it down,
If the weather'd be sunny or stormy.

Well, wouldn't you know it?
    they put me on drag,
But *my secret* nobody found out,
For I's destined to choke
    on their jibes, and their jokes
And the names them cow punchers
    would sound out.

So I kept my mouth shut
    as the years rumbled by --
By then I'd made lookout and point;
Boy, what you can get
    with sweat, blood, and more sweat;
Why, I ended up ownin' the joint!

So now I'm the boss,
    and my hair's turnin' gray,
And it seemed the charade should be endin';
It shouldn't affect me;
    they've got to respect me!
There's no use to go on pretendin'.

———➤

Now I watch the cook's lad
    with that big coffee pot --
Me, he serves with respect
    and with deference.
As my back gathers moss,
    after all, I'm the boss,
I've a *right* to be statin' my *preference!*

So I stood up and spoke up
    real clearly and loud,
So they all of 'em heard and could see,
And then in my best western
    John Wayne type drawl,
I said, *"Son, you can make mine **tea!**"*

ΩΩΩΩΩ

... *Dee Strickland Johnson,* © *March, 1996*

THE BLIND COWBOY
(To my friend Bill Endicott, who knows)

My days in the saddle are over,
    and I know that my cowboying is done;
But I still feel the space; winter wind on my face,
    warm spring rains, and the hot summer sun.
This big silver buckle means *champion*
  calf roper for some by-gone year,
And my fingers can trace
    an old trophy's *"First Place"*--
Team tying some rangy old steer.

I still kind of thrill to the texture
    of my coiled rope right here by my chair,
And time can't efface all the memories that race
    through my mind, just as close as the air.
Some tell me there once lived a deaf man
    who composed in a silence like night;
Well, I wish that I could, but I ain't that good
  -- still, just *singing* sure don't require *sight*.

So I sing, and I fiddle with fiddles,
    and I whistle and play the old tunes
      to which I used to dance
    in the days of my youth,
And I reckon that I still commune
  with sights, sounds,
 and scents of the old days,
  for I yodel and hum as I ride
      the dim dusty trails of my mem'ries
        with that slip of a girl by my side

Where the wind sings its song in the sagebrush,
    and a lizard streaks off through the grass.
The cattle are lowing,
    the cloud shadows growing,
    and I pray that they never will pass.

———▶

Old friends from the ranches are gone now,
    but it seems I can still hear their spurs.
A boot scrapes and talks
    from old wooden sidewalks;
        And the voices -- I can't forget *hers*!

How lovely, how sweet was her singing!
    How quickly the hours slipped away
As together we sang, and the harmony rang
    at the end of each tiring day.
And her face. Those eyes seem to haunt me
    as they did when they looked into mine,
As we dallied and stayed and two fiddles played
    by the trail midst the blue columbine.

But I can still sing in the Springtime,
    be it summer or winter or fall.
It's all moving smoke,
    and my voice seems to choke
        on the words of the simplest song;
I may choose to ride in the moonlight,
    though it really be noonday or dawn,
And this grassy old rope
    still tells me there's hope --
        and it gives me the strength to go on.

ΩΩΩΩΩ

    . . . *Dee Strickland Johnson,* © *July, 1997*

"Bill's Boots"

END OF THE DAY

Well, I see that the sun is setting,
    and quite soon the day will be gone,
But it doesn't much disturb me,
    'cause there'll sure be another dawn.

See, a cowboy lives in the country
    where he watches the seasons change.
One just comes after the other,
    and away out here on the range
Its roundup and brand in the springtime,
    Haul water in June and July.

In fall, its roundup and shipping;
    then gather in a supply
        of firewood and feed for the cattle,
For winter is harsh beyond doubt;
    but always, there's greenup in Springtime
'Cause somebody planned it all out.

Drought may well bring disaster;
    Yet I know *sometime* it will rain.
A cloudburst can mean misfortune;
    But the sun will shine someday again.

My sunset is quickly approaching;
    my evening star's brightening up there;
But I'm sure the designer of nature,
    is preparing a dawning -- somewhere.

ΩΩΩΩΩ

        . . . *Dee Strickland Johnson, © July 1997*

Index

At The Dance	36
Blind Cowboy, The	59
Boston Horse Trader, The	32
Cowboy Goes A-Courtin'	51
Cowboy Poetry: Out of Style	26
Dark Eyed Stranger, The	8
Déjà Vu	12
End of the Day	62
First Roundup	30
Fredonia	24
Morning in the High Hills	20
My Blue Eyed Anna Beth	22
My Buddy	44
My Vanishing Boots and Hats	50
Not Quite Lost Weekend	10
Passing of a Cowboy, The	54
Queen of Spades, The	14
Quiet Man, The	17
Rawhide Annie	11
Really Rich Rancher, The	38
Secret, The	56
Taming of Wild Cat Willie, The	34
These Boots *Ain't* Made for Walkin'	47
Tom's Truck	40
Winds of the West	21

Illustrations

Frontispiece	*Troy Strickland*
6	*Tim*
14	*Jolene*
16	*Daniel*
18	*Roxane*
28	*Self Portrait*
46	*Jon and Becky*
53	*Cephas and Josie*
61	*Bill Endicott's Boots*

About the Author

Dee Strickland Johnson is a native of Arizona. She lived the early years of her life on the Navajo and Hualapai reservations and at the Petrified Forest. In the 1970's she and her husband John operated a small cattle ranch in Arkansas. There, Dee and their three children were involved in the musical shows at the Ozark Folk Center. Dee has retired from teaching American history in high school. Cowboy music, poetry, and art continue to occupy much of her time, and she appears at Cowboy Gatherings around the country. Her first book is called Cowman's Wife.

Photo by Ken Clemmer